Baby Jesus ABC Story-book

Illustrated by Cecile Lamb

ISBN: 0-87239-354-2

 STANDARD PUBLISHING

Cincinnati, Ohio   3624

Long ago, in a town far away, an ANGEL brought a message from God to a young woman named Mary.

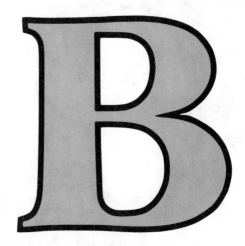

The Angel's message was this: "God is going to send you a BABY. He will be God's own Son."

Mary and Joseph went on a journey from Nazareth to Bethlehem, which was called the CITY of David.

The travelers walked for many miles. Mary rode on a DONKEY, and Joseph walked beside her.

In Bethlehem at last, Mary and Joseph rested. That night the promised baby came to EARTH.

Shepherds were watching their FLOCKS of sheep on the hills near Bethlehem, in the quiet night.

Suddenly the shepherds saw many angels in the sky. They sang, "GLORY, glory, glory to God!"

H

The HEAVENS were filled with the singing. One angel told the shepherds they might go see the baby.

The shepherds hurried to Bethlehem. In the stable of an INN they
found the baby, and worshiped Him.

"JESUS is His name," Mary told the shepherds softly. "God has given us a wonderful, wonderful gift."

"He is a KING. He is the Son of God," the shepherds said. "His kingdom shall last forever."

"He is the King of LOVE. He came to show us God's love. He will teach all people to love."

M

The baby's bed was a MANGER. The
King of Love was born in the stable
with the sleepy animals nearby.

"Good NEWS!" the shepherds told the people of Bethlehem. "A baby has been born! Good NEWS!"

OLD and young rejoiced to hear that baby Jesus had been born. God gave the baby to them all.

Perhaps the people of Bethlehem
brought the new baby PRESENTS to
show their love and thanks to God.

And the shepherds returned to their QUIET hills, to think about all that had happened.

Meanwhile, wise RULERS in a far-away country had found out about the birth of a new baby king.

A STAR showed these men of the East that a king had been born. They had been watching for the sign.

So the men got on their camels and TRAVELED many days and nights to find the young king and worship Him.

They looked UP and followed wherever the star led them. When the star stopped, they stopped, too.

Over the VILLAGE of Bethlehem the
star stood still. "Is there a king in
this small town?" the men asked.

The WISE-MEN went into the house
the star shone upon. And there they
found the little baby Jesus.

The Wise-men rejoiced with EXCEEDING great joy, because they had at last found God's great gift.

The Wise-men gave the YOUNG king gifts of gold, and frankincense, and myrrh, and worshiped Him.

Z-Z-Z-Z the village slept; the whole world slept. Peace and love had come to all people on Christmas.